EMMANUEL JOSEPH

The Spiritual Player, Exploring Education and Gaming as Paths to Inner Discovery

Copyright © 2025 by Emmanuel Joseph

All rights reserved. No part of this publication may be reproduced, stored or transmitted in any form or by any means, electronic, mechanical, photocopying, recording, scanning, or otherwise without written permission from the publisher. It is illegal to copy this book, post it to a website, or distribute it by any other means without permission.

First edition

This book was professionally typeset on Reedsy. Find out more at reedsy.com

Contents

1	Chapter 1: The Awakening of the Mind	1
2	Chapter 2: The Quest for Knowledge	3
3	Chapter 3: The Role of Mentorship	5
4	Chapter 4: The Power of Community	7
5	Chapter 5: The Intersection of Creativity and Learning	9
6	Chapter 6: The Balance of Discipline and Play	11
7	Chapter 7: The Role of Reflection	13
8	Chapter 8: The Influence of Technology	15
9	Chapter 9: The Impact of Competition	17
10	Chapter 10: The Role of Failure	19
11	Chapter 11: The Pursuit of Mastery	21
12	Chapter 12: The Path to Inner Discovery	23
13	Chapter 13: The Journey of Emotional Intelligence	25
14	Chapter 14: The Influence of Cultural Diversity	27
15	Chapter 15: The Power of Mindfulness	29

1

Chapter 1: The Awakening of the Mind

The journey of self-discovery often begins with the awakening of the mind. Education plays a pivotal role in this process, acting as the catalyst that sparks curiosity and ignites the flame of knowledge. In traditional settings, education is perceived merely as the acquisition of information. However, a deeper understanding reveals that it is also a means to explore one's inner self. This chapter delves into the transformative power of education, illustrating how it helps individuals to understand their strengths, weaknesses, and unique abilities.

In the realm of gaming, a similar awakening occurs. Video games, often dismissed as mere entertainment, have the potential to foster cognitive and emotional growth. Gamers develop problem-solving skills, strategic thinking, and resilience through their virtual experiences. The challenges and quests in games parallel real-life obstacles, offering players a safe environment to test their limits and expand their horizons. This chapter examines the parallels between education and gaming, demonstrating how both can lead to profound personal growth.

The connection between education and gaming becomes evident when one considers the concept of learning through play. This approach emphasizes experiential learning, where individuals actively engage in tasks that stimulate their intellect and creativity. Whether in a classroom or a virtual world, the principles of learning through play remain consistent. By embracing this philosophy, individuals can unlock their potential and embark on a path of self-discovery.

Ultimately, the awakening of the mind is not confined to a specific medium. It transcends traditional boundaries, encompassing a wide range of experiences and interactions. This chapter highlights the importance of maintaining an open mind and embracing diverse avenues for growth. Whether through formal education or immersive gaming experiences, the journey to inner discovery begins with the awakening of the mind.

2

Chapter 2: The Quest for Knowledge

The quest for knowledge is a lifelong pursuit that transcends the confines of academia. Education, in its purest form, is a relentless journey toward understanding the world and oneself. This chapter explores the various stages of this quest, emphasizing the significance of curiosity and the desire to learn. It highlights how education fosters intellectual growth, enabling individuals to navigate the complexities of life with confidence and wisdom.

In the gaming world, quests are central to the player's experience. These virtual adventures mirror the real-life pursuit of knowledge, as players embark on missions to uncover hidden truths and solve intricate puzzles. The immersive nature of gaming allows individuals to experience the thrill of discovery and the satisfaction of overcoming challenges. This chapter delves into the parallels between educational quests and gaming quests, illustrating how both can inspire a sense of wonder and achievement.

The intersection of education and gaming becomes apparent when one considers the concept of gamification. By incorporating game-like elements into educational settings, learners are motivated to engage more deeply with the material. This approach not only makes learning more enjoyable but also enhances retention and comprehension. This chapter examines the benefits of gamification, providing examples of how it can be effectively integrated into various educational contexts.

Ultimately, the quest for knowledge is a dynamic and multifaceted journey. It requires individuals to remain curious and open-minded, continually seeking new experiences and insights. Whether through traditional education or immersive gaming, the pursuit of knowledge is a fundamental aspect of personal growth and inner discovery. This chapter emphasizes the importance of embracing this journey, recognizing that the quest for knowledge is both an individual and collective endeavor.

3

Chapter 3: The Role of Mentorship

Mentorship is a critical component of both education and gaming, providing guidance and support to individuals on their path to self-discovery. In educational settings, mentors serve as role models, offering wisdom and encouragement to help students navigate their academic and personal challenges. This chapter explores the various forms of mentorship, highlighting the importance of fostering meaningful connections between mentors and mentees.

In the gaming world, mentorship takes on a unique form. Experienced players often guide newcomers, sharing their knowledge and strategies to help them succeed. This sense of community and collaboration is essential for personal growth, as it encourages individuals to learn from one another and develop their skills. This chapter examines the impact of mentorship in gaming, illustrating how it fosters a sense of belonging and mutual respect.

The parallels between mentorship in education and gaming are evident when one considers the role of teachers and coaches. Both provide valuable insights and feedback, helping individuals to refine their abilities and achieve their goals. By fostering a supportive environment, mentors in both contexts can inspire confidence and resilience in their mentees. This chapter delves into the qualities of effective mentors, emphasizing the importance of empathy, patience, and adaptability.

Ultimately, mentorship is a reciprocal relationship that benefits both parties.

Mentors gain a sense of fulfillment from helping others, while mentees receive the guidance and support they need to thrive. This chapter underscores the significance of mentorship in the journey to inner discovery, highlighting how it can positively impact individuals in both educational and gaming contexts. By fostering strong mentor-mentee relationships, individuals can achieve greater self-awareness and personal growth.

4

Chapter 4: The Power of Community

Community plays a vital role in both education and gaming, providing individuals with a sense of belonging and support. In educational settings, communities are formed through shared experiences and common goals. This chapter explores the importance of community in fostering a positive learning environment, highlighting how collaboration and teamwork can enhance personal growth.

In the gaming world, communities are often built around shared interests and virtual spaces. These digital communities provide a platform for players to connect, share experiences, and support one another. The sense of camaraderie and mutual respect that develops within these communities is essential for personal development. This chapter examines the impact of gaming communities on individuals, illustrating how they foster a sense of belonging and empowerment.

The intersection of community in education and gaming becomes apparent when one considers the concept of collaborative learning. By working together, individuals can leverage their collective knowledge and skills to achieve common goals. This approach not only enhances learning outcomes but also fosters a sense of unity and cooperation. This chapter delves into the benefits of collaborative learning, providing examples of how it can be effectively implemented in various contexts.

Ultimately, the power of community lies in its ability to bring people together and create a supportive environment for personal growth. Whether in educational settings or virtual gaming spaces, communities provide individuals with the encouragement and resources they need to succeed. This chapter emphasizes the importance of fostering strong communities, recognizing that they play a crucial role in the journey to inner discovery.

5

Chapter 5: The Intersection of Creativity and Learning

Creativity is a fundamental aspect of both education and gaming, allowing individuals to express themselves and explore new ideas. In educational settings, creativity fosters innovation and critical thinking, enabling students to approach problems from unique perspectives. This chapter explores the role of creativity in education, highlighting how it can enhance learning outcomes and personal growth.

In the gaming world, creativity is often at the forefront of the player's experience. Game design and storytelling provide a platform for individuals to immerse themselves in imaginative worlds and create their own narratives. This chapter examines the impact of creativity in gaming, illustrating how it fosters cognitive and emotional development. By encouraging players to think outside the box, gaming can inspire new ways of thinking and problem-solving.

The intersection of creativity and learning becomes evident when one considers the concept of project-based learning. This approach emphasizes hands-on, experiential learning, where individuals actively engage in tasks that stimulate their intellect and creativity. Whether in a classroom or a virtual world, the principles of project-based learning remain consistent. This chapter delves into the benefits of this approach, providing examples of how it can be effectively integrated into various educational and gaming contexts.

Ultimately, the fusion of creativity and learning is essential for personal growth and inner discovery. By embracing creative endeavors, individuals can unlock their potential and explore new possibilities. This chapter underscores the importance of nurturing creativity in both educational and gaming settings, recognizing that it plays a crucial role in the journey to self-discovery.

6

Chapter 6: The Balance of Discipline and Play

Discipline and play are often seen as opposing forces, but they are both essential for personal growth. In educational settings, discipline fosters focus and perseverance, enabling individuals to achieve their goals. This chapter explores the importance of discipline in education, highlighting how it can enhance learning outcomes and personal development.

In the gaming world, play is central to the player's experience. It provides a platform for individuals to explore, experiment, and have fun. This chapter examines the role of play in gaming, illustrating how it fosters creativity, resilience, and problem-solving skills. By engaging in playful activities, individuals can develop a growth mindset and a sense of curiosity.

The balance of discipline and play becomes evident when one considers the concept of structured play. This approach emphasizes the importance of setting boundaries and goals while allowing for creativity and exploration. By finding a balance between discipline and play, individuals can maximize their potential and achieve a sense of fulfillment. This chapter delves into the benefits of structured play, providing examples of how it can be effectively integrated into various educational and gaming contexts.

Ultimately, the balance of discipline and play is essential for personal growth and inner discovery. By embracing both aspects, individuals can develop a well-rounded approach to life and learning. This chapter underscores the importance of finding this balance, recognizing that it plays a crucial role in the journey to self-discovery.

7

Chapter 7: The Role of Reflection

Reflection is a critical component of both education and gaming, providing individuals with the opportunity to evaluate their experiences and learn from them. In educational settings, reflection fosters self-awareness and critical thinking, enabling individuals to gain insights into their strengths and weaknesses. This chapter explores the importance of reflection in education, highlighting how it can enhance personal growth and learning outcomes.

In the gaming world, reflection is often an integral part of the player's experience. After completing a challenge or quest, players are encouraged to reflect on their performance and identify areas for improvement. This chapter examines the role of reflection in gaming, illustrating how it fosters cognitive and emotional development. By reflecting on their experiences, players can develop a deeper understanding of themselves and their abilities.

The intersection of reflection in education and gaming becomes apparent when one considers the concept of metacognition. This practice involves thinking about one's thinking, allowing individuals to gain insights into their cognitive processes and improve their learning strategies. By incorporating metacognitive practices into educational and gaming contexts, individuals can enhance their self-awareness and personal growth. This chapter delves into the benefits of reflection and metacognition, providing examples of how they can be effectively integrated into various settings.

Ultimately, reflection is a powerful tool for personal growth and inner discovery. By taking the time to evaluate their experiences and learn from them, individuals can develop a deeper understanding of themselves and their abilities. This chapter underscores the importance of reflection in both educational and gaming settings, recognizing that it plays a crucial role in the journey to self-discovery.

8

Chapter 8: The Influence of Technology

Technology has a profound impact on both education and gaming, shaping the way individuals learn and interact with the world. In educational settings, technology enhances the accessibility and efficiency of learning, providing students with a wealth of resources at their fingertips. This chapter explores the role of technology in education, highlighting how it can enhance learning outcomes and personal growth.

In the gaming world, technology is at the forefront of the player's experience. Advances in graphics, artificial intelligence, and virtual reality create immersive environments that captivate players and foster cognitive and emotional development. This chapter examines the influence of technology in gaming, illustrating how it can enhance the player's experience and facilitate personal growth.

The intersection of technology in education and gaming becomes evident when one considers the concept of blended learning. This approach combines traditional face-to-face instruction with digital tools and resources, creating a more flexible and engaging learning environment. By leveraging the strengths of both mediums, blended learning can enhance student outcomes and foster a sense of curiosity and innovation. This chapter delves into the benefits of blended learning, providing examples of how it can be effectively integrated into various educational and gaming contexts.

Ultimately, technology is a powerful tool that can enhance both education and gaming experiences. By embracing technological advancements, individuals can unlock new possibilities for learning and personal growth. This chapter underscores the importance of leveraging technology in the journey to self-discovery, recognizing that it plays a crucial role in shaping the future of education and gaming.

9

Chapter 9: The Impact of Competition

Competition is a common element in both education and gaming, driving individuals to strive for excellence and achieve their goals. In educational settings, competition can motivate students to perform at their best and develop a sense of discipline and resilience. This chapter explores the role of competition in education, highlighting how it can enhance learning outcomes and personal growth.

In the gaming world, competition is often at the heart of the player's experience. Whether through multiplayer games or leaderboards, players are driven to improve their skills and achieve high scores. This chapter examines the impact of competition in gaming, illustrating how it can foster cognitive and emotional development. By engaging in competitive activities, players can develop a growth mindset and a sense of determination.

The intersection of competition in education and gaming becomes apparent when one considers the concept of healthy competition. This approach emphasizes the importance of fostering a positive and supportive environment where individuals can challenge themselves and others in a constructive manner. By promoting healthy competition, individuals can develop a sense of camaraderie and mutual respect. This chapter delves into the benefits of healthy competition, providing examples of how it can be effectively integrated into various educational and gaming contexts.

Ultimately, competition is a powerful motivator that can drive personal growth and inner discovery. By embracing competitive activities, individuals can develop a sense of discipline, resilience, and determination. This chapter underscores the importance of fostering healthy competition in both educational and gaming settings, recognizing that it plays a crucial role in the journey to self-discovery.

10

Chapter 10: The Role of Failure

Failure is an inevitable part of both education and gaming, providing valuable learning opportunities and fostering personal growth. In educational settings, failure can help students develop resilience and perseverance, enabling them to overcome challenges and achieve their goals. This chapter explores the importance of failure in education, highlighting how it can enhance learning outcomes and personal development.

In the gaming world, failure is often an integral part of the player's experience. Players frequently encounter obstacles and setbacks, requiring them to develop problem-solving skills and adaptability. This chapter examines the role of failure in gaming, illustrating how it can foster cognitive and emotional development. By embracing failure as a learning opportunity, players can develop a growth mindset and a sense of determination.

The intersection of failure in education and gaming becomes apparent when one considers the concept of failing forward. This approach emphasizes the importance of learning from mistakes and using them as stepping stones to success. By fostering a positive attitude towards failure, individuals can develop resilience and a sense of curiosity. This chapter delves into the benefits of failing forward, providing examples of how it can be effectively integrated into various educational and gaming contexts.

Ultimately, failure is a powerful tool for personal growth and inner discovery. By embracing failure as a learning opportunity, individuals can develop a deeper understanding of themselves and their abilities. This chapter underscores the importance of fostering a positive attitude towards failure in both educational and gaming settings, recognizing that it plays a crucial role in the journey to self-discovery.

11

Chapter 11: The Pursuit of Mastery

Mastery is the ultimate goal of both education and gaming, representing the culmination of one's efforts and dedication. In educational settings, the pursuit of mastery involves developing a deep understanding of a subject and the ability to apply knowledge effectively. This chapter explores the importance of mastery in education, highlighting how it can enhance learning outcomes and personal growth.

In the gaming world, the pursuit of mastery is often at the heart of the player's experience. Players strive to hone their skills and achieve high levels of proficiency in their chosen games. This chapter examines the role of mastery in gaming, illustrating how it can foster cognitive and emotional development. By pursuing mastery, players can develop a sense of discipline, resilience, and self-confidence.

The intersection of mastery in education and gaming becomes apparent when one considers the concept of deliberate practice. This approach emphasizes the importance of focused and intentional practice, where individuals actively seek to improve their skills and knowledge. By incorporating deliberate practice into educational and gaming contexts, individuals can achieve higher levels of mastery and personal growth. This chapter delves into the benefits of deliberate practice, providing examples of how it can be effectively integrated into various settings.

Ultimately, the pursuit of mastery is a lifelong journey that requires dedication, perseverance, and a growth mindset. By embracing the quest for mastery, individuals can unlock their potential and achieve a sense of fulfillment. This chapter underscores the importance of pursuing mastery in both educational and gaming settings, recognizing that it plays a crucial role in the journey to self-discovery.

12

Chapter 12: The Path to Inner Discovery

The journey to inner discovery is a multifaceted and dynamic process that involves exploration, reflection, and growth. Education and gaming both provide valuable avenues for this journey, offering unique opportunities for individuals to develop their cognitive, emotional, and social skills. This chapter explores the various stages of inner discovery, highlighting the importance of maintaining an open mind and embracing diverse experiences.

In educational settings, the path to inner discovery involves developing a deep understanding of oneself and the world. This process requires individuals to engage in critical thinking, self-reflection, and meaningful interactions with others. This chapter examines the role of education in fostering inner discovery, illustrating how it can enhance personal growth and self-awareness.

In the gaming world, the path to inner discovery is often intertwined with the player's virtual experiences. Through immersive gameplay and interactive storytelling, players can explore new perspectives, challenge their assumptions, and develop a deeper understanding of themselves. This chapter delves into the impact of gaming on inner discovery, providing examples of how it can foster cognitive and emotional development.

Ultimately, the path to inner discovery is a lifelong journey that requires individuals to remain curious, open-minded, and resilient. By embracing the opportunities provided by both education and gaming, individuals can unlock their potential and achieve a sense of fulfillment. This chapter underscores the importance of maintaining a balanced and holistic approach to personal growth, recognizing that the journey to inner discovery is both an individual and collective endeavor.

13

Chapter 13: The Journey of Emotional Intelligence

Emotional intelligence is a crucial aspect of both education and gaming, enabling individuals to navigate their emotions and develop meaningful relationships. In educational settings, emotional intelligence fosters self-awareness, empathy, and effective communication. This chapter explores the importance of emotional intelligence in education, highlighting how it can enhance personal growth and interpersonal skills.

In the gaming world, emotional intelligence is often developed through interactive storytelling and character development. Players are encouraged to empathize with characters, make moral decisions, and navigate complex social dynamics. This chapter examines the role of emotional intelligence in gaming, illustrating how it fosters cognitive and emotional development. By engaging in emotionally rich experiences, players can develop a deeper understanding of themselves and others.

The intersection of emotional intelligence in education and gaming becomes apparent when one considers the concept of social and emotional learning (SEL). This approach emphasizes the importance of developing emotional and social skills alongside academic knowledge. By incorporating SEL into educational and gaming contexts, individuals can achieve greater personal growth and emotional well-being. This chapter delves into the benefits of SEL, providing examples of how it can be effectively integrated into various settings.

Ultimately, emotional intelligence is a powerful tool for personal growth and inner discovery. By developing emotional awareness and empathy, individuals can navigate their emotions and build meaningful relationships. This chapter underscores the importance of fostering emotional intelligence in both educational and gaming settings, recognizing that it plays a crucial role in the journey to self-discovery.

14

Chapter 14: The Influence of Cultural Diversity

Cultural diversity enriches both education and gaming, providing individuals with diverse perspectives and experiences. In educational settings, cultural diversity fosters a deeper understanding of the world and promotes inclusivity and respect. This chapter explores the importance of cultural diversity in education, highlighting how it can enhance personal growth and global awareness.

In the gaming world, cultural diversity is often reflected in the characters, narratives, and settings of games. Players are exposed to diverse cultures, traditions, and worldviews, fostering a sense of curiosity and empathy. This chapter examines the impact of cultural diversity in gaming, illustrating how it can enhance the player's experience and foster cognitive and emotional development. By embracing cultural diversity, players can develop a broader understanding of the world and their place within it.

The intersection of cultural diversity in education and gaming becomes evident when one considers the concept of multicultural education. This approach emphasizes the importance of incorporating diverse perspectives and experiences into the curriculum. By promoting multicultural education, individuals can develop a sense of global citizenship and inclusivity. This chapter delves into the benefits of multicultural education, providing examples of how it can be effectively integrated into various educational and gaming contexts.

Ultimately, cultural diversity is a powerful tool for personal growth and inner discovery. By embracing diverse perspectives and experiences, individuals can develop a deeper understanding of themselves and the world. This chapter underscores the importance of fostering cultural diversity in both educational and gaming settings, recognizing that it plays a crucial role in the journey to self-discovery.

15

Chapter 15: The Power of Mindfulness

Mindfulness is a fundamental aspect of both education and gaming, enabling individuals to focus on the present moment and develop a sense of inner peace. In educational settings, mindfulness fosters concentration, self-regulation, and emotional well-being. This chapter explores the importance of mindfulness in education, highlighting how it can enhance personal growth and learning outcomes.

In the gaming world, mindfulness is often developed through immersive gameplay and interactive experiences. Players are encouraged to focus on the present moment, develop strategies, and navigate challenges mindfully. This chapter examines the role of mindfulness in gaming, illustrating how it fosters cognitive and emotional development. By engaging in mindful activities, players can develop a deeper sense of self-awareness and inner calm.

The intersection of mindfulness in education and gaming becomes apparent when one considers the concept of mindful learning. This approach emphasizes the importance of being fully present and engaged in the learning process. By incorporating mindful learning into educational and gaming contexts, individuals can achieve greater personal growth and emotional well-being. This chapter delves into the benefits of mindful learning, providing examples of how it can be effectively integrated into various settings.

Ultimately, mindfulness is a powerful tool for personal growth and inner discovery. By developing a sense of presence and inner calm, individuals can navigate their emotions and experiences more effectively. This chapter underscores the importance of fostering mindfulness in both educational and gaming settings, recognizing that it plays a crucial role in the journey to self-discovery.

The Spiritual Player: Exploring Education and Gaming as Paths to Inner Discovery

In a world where education and gaming are often seen as separate spheres, *The Spiritual Player* bridges the gap to reveal their profound intersections. This enlightening book takes readers on a transformative journey, uncovering how both educational pursuits and gaming adventures can serve as powerful paths to self-discovery.

Through twelve captivating chapters, the book delves into the essence of learning, creativity, community, and resilience. It explores how the quest for knowledge and the thrill of gaming quests foster cognitive and emotional growth, offering unique opportunities for personal development. Readers will discover the vital role of mentorship, the power of community, and the balance of discipline and play in shaping their inner selves.

With insightful reflections on the importance of failure, the pursuit of mastery, and the impact of cultural diversity, *The Spiritual Player* provides a holistic approach to inner discovery. It highlights the significance of emotional intelligence, mindfulness, and technological advancements in enhancing both educational and gaming experiences.

Drawing from the intersections of education and gaming, this book offers a fresh perspective on personal growth. It encourages readers to embrace curiosity, resilience, and empathy as they navigate their journeys toward inner discovery. Whether you are an educator, gamer, or seeker of self-awareness, *The Spiritual Player* invites you to embark on a transformative journey that transcends traditional boundaries and unveils the interconnectedness of learning and play.

www.ingramcontent.com/pod-product-compliance
Lightning Source LLC
LaVergne TN
LVHW010444070526
838199LV00066B/6176